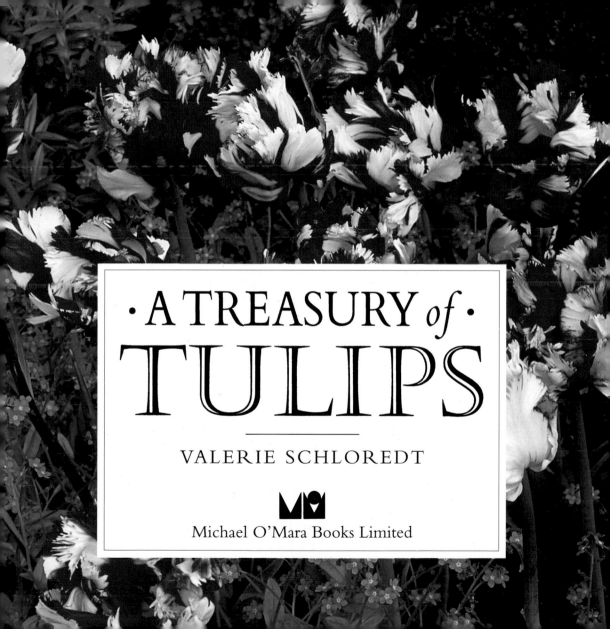

· A TREASURY *of* ·
TULIPS

VALERIE SCHLOREDT

Michael O'Mara Books Limited

Flowers are in short supply during the bare months of winter. The tulip is among the first to make its appearance at the beginning of spring – and what more encouraging sight is there after the cold dark days than the brilliant splashes of colour made by masses of tulips in our parks and gardens?

Tulips are the stalwarts of the garden, surviving over the chilliest winters, and thriving in the cool rain and brisk breezes of early spring that discourage less hardy specimens. Perhaps because it performs so faithfully, few people realize that the garden tulip began its career as a precious symbol of luxury. It was first cultivated in the royal gardens of Persia and the Ottoman empire.

The flower
was much admired after
it was brought to Europe in the
16th century and at one point tulips became
so valuable that they were traded for fabulous prices on
the Dutch stock exchange.

The types of tulips that were grown in Holland 400 years ago were
more fragile and less dependable than the sturdy varieties we grow in our
gardens today. Modern hybrids have been bred for reliability, and also
offer a cornucopia of shapes, colours and sizes to choose from. At present,
approximately 800 tulip varieties are commercially available. Shapes range
from the elegant lily-flowered tulips to the pleasingly simple Darwins, the
voluptuous double-blossomed varieties, and the eccentric fringed petals of
the parrot tulips. There are myriad colours to enjoy: pure white and pastel
pink, bright oranges and yellows, all shades of red from rose to scarlet, and
dark dusky purples. Patterning may be a simple blush, an outline at the tip

of a petal, or stripes and swirling streaks. The tulip has inspired artists throughout its history. It was a favourite subject of the great Dutch flower painters of the 17th and 18th centuries, and appears repeatedly in different forms as a decorative motif on furniture, carpets, glass, ceramics and fabric designs.

Tulips also appeal to the artistic gardener. They can be used in the garden the way paint is used on canvas, in great swathes or tiny spots of colour. Let this book be your inspiration for the tulip, a true garden treasure.

WHAT IS A TULIP?

A member of the lily family, the tulip is a bulbous plant which grows roots over winter, sends up a shoot which flowers in spring, and uses its leaves to produce nutrients which are stored in the bulb over the summer.

By the time the leaves have died down, it has produced one 'daughter' bulb for the next season, as well as several immature offset bulbs. In this way, many identical flowers are grown from one original bulb – a much quicker process than reproduction from seed, which takes six years to produce a mature flowering plant.

Genetic mutations, or 'sports', arise frequently, and cross-fertilization is also easily achieved. This variability has given rise to a bewildering array of tulip varieties. To simplify matters, garden hybrids are classified as 'earlies', 'mid-seasons' and 'lates'.

THE WILD TULIP

It all began with the 'primitive' or wild tulips native to Western and Central Asia, where they thrive in mountainous areas on rocky hillsides and in alpine meadows. The wild tulip is well adapted for life in the region. It needs sharply-drained soil and spring showers, but can tolerate baking hot summers and frozen winters.

How and when these wild tulips were first cultivated is unknown, but we know tulips were grown in the gardens of the Persian court as far back as the 13th century, when they are mentioned in poetry. The conquering Ottoman Turks inherited the Persian slave gardeners, as well as their techniques for growing tulips. The first tulips sent to Europe were the product of these centuries of cultivation. European florists immediately set about experimenting with the flower, cross-breeding garden tulips with wild tulips imported from Asia.

Dutch bulb companies continued the process. Expeditions were sent to search the remote foothills of Central Asia for new 'botanical tulips' until the outbreak of the First World War.

THE DISCOVERY
OF THE TULIP

Cultivated tulips were unknown in Europe until the 16th century, when they were first 'discovered' by Europeans visiting the East.

The Austrian ambassador to the Ottoman court was one such visitor. Ogier Ghiselin de Busbecq journeyed across northern Turkey to Constantinople in 1554, and wrote of the astonishing flowers, blooming in mid-winter, he had seen along the way: 'those that the Turks call tulipam are admired for the beauty and variety of their colours. The Turks pay great attention to the cultivation of flowers, and do not hesitate to pay several aspers for one that is beautiful.'

Busbecq sent bulbs and seeds back to Vienna and from there they were passed on as high-priced novelties.

The botanist Carol Clusius became famous for growing tulips in the horticultural gardens at Leiden in Holland. He was approached by entrepreneurs who recognized the flower's profit-making potential, but he refused to sell. Unfortunately for Clusius, he lost some of his best specimens to thieves and these stolen bulbs were eventually propagated and sold across Holland.

TULIPMANIA

The connection between Holland and tulips has endured for 400 years, since the first bulbs planted in Leiden blossomed in the spring of 1594. The tulip soon became fashionable across Europe. In the French court, ladies wore tulips rather than jewels, and in the newly prosperous Dutch Republic wealthy merchants gave tulips pride of place in their showpiece gardens.

Tulips became a national obsession in Holland, and prices soared when the Dutch stock market was swept up in the craze. At the height of 'tulipmania' in 1636, one single bulb of the Viceroy variety was sold for goods to the value of 2,500 florins – including two loads of wheat, four loads of rye, four fat oxen, eight pigs, twelve sheep, a thousand pounds of cheese, four barrels of beer, a suit of clothes and a bed. Many speculators were ruined when prices suddenly dropped and the tulip market collapsed.

The frivolities of tulipmania were further deflated by the Napoleonic wars. A more sober attitude to the trade was established and the bulb business in Holland began to develop into the solid professional industry that it remains today.

TULIPS IN TURKEY

Although the tulip was long a royal emblem of the Ottoman court, 'tulipmania' did not arrive in Turkey until the 18th century, when the flower was already well established in Europe.

By the reign of Ahmed III (1703 – 30), the Ottoman Empire was in decline and the Sultan's court was given up to pleasure at the expense of affairs of state. The Grand Vizier Mehmed, the Sultan's chief minister, was chief steward of the royal tulips. Every spring he held for the Sultan's pleasure a great tulip festival when the royal gardens were alive with more than half a million tulips.

At night, there were tulip parties and guests strolled through the moonlight

dressed to complement the flowers. Thousands of candles in globes of tinted glass flickered among the tulips and in the trees hung cages of song birds. Only when the last tulip petal fell was the festival ended.

The Vizier Mehmed, 'Lalézare' the tulip lover, wrote a book listing 1323 varieties of tulip. He favoured almond-shaped tulips like these portrayed on 15th century Iznik tiles from the Sultan's palace, the Topkapisaray.

And, such being used in Eastern bowers,
Young maids may wonder if the flowers
Or meanings be the sweeter.

FROM 'A Flower in a Letter'
BY ELIZABETH BARRETT BROWNING (1806–61)

TULIPS

Let tulips trust not the warm vernal rain,
But dread the frosts and still their blooms restrain;
So when bright Phoebus smiles with kindly care,
The moon not sullied by a lowering air,
Early the beauteous race you'll wondering see,
Ranged in the beds, a numerous progeny:
The tulip with her painted charm display
Throughout the mild air, and make the garden gay;
The tulip which with gaudy colours stained,
The name of beauty to her race has gained,
For whether she in scarlet does delight,
Chequered and streaked with lines of glittering white,
Or sprinkled o'er with purple charms our sight;
Or window-like beneath a sable veil,
Her purest lawn does artfully conceal,
Or emulate, the varied agate's veins,
From every flower the beauty's prize obtained.

ABRAHAM COWLEY (1618-67)

TULIPS IN ART

Although wild tulips grow today in Italy and Spain, botanists believe they were naturalized after tulips were brought to Europe from Turkey in the 16th century. Yet some surviving examples of medieval European art show the tulip long before the actual flower was known in Europe.

The artist who decorated an illuminated Italian Bible of the 12th century with a tulip motif must have been influenced by tulips in art imported from Turkey or Persia. A similar mystery clouds the origins of the tulips that surround the Madonna and Child in a 15th century mural from Coventry Cathedral. It was hidden by the building work of subsequent centuries, and only discovered after the cathedral was bombed during the Second World War.

After they were imported to Europe, tulips fascinated artists both for their beauty and as a symbol of luxury. Some of the finest flower illustrations of the 17th century were created to advertise tulips in bulb catalogues. They provide an accurate

picture of the flower in all its particulars – bulb, root, leaf and even accompanying insect life!

There are also many depictions of tulips as a fashionable garden flower. Peter Paul Rubens (1577-1640) painted his young wife Hélène Fourment in her garden, where tulips grew in well-ordered formal beds.

The flower paintings so popular in the 18th century usually included tulips. Rather than painting an actual bouquet from life, artists would paint a flower or two at a time – tulips, irises, roses – as they came into season. With their twisting stems and loose blossoms, these still life tulips capture the drama of the moment just before the petals fall and the flower dies.

'BROKEN' TULIPS

Tulips with a streaked effect, the background colour broken by delicate strokes of another colour, were highly prized by the Dutch in the 17th century. 'Semper Augustus' and 'Viceroy' were two varieties of 'broken' or 'florist's' tulips which fetched fabulous prices on the Dutch stock market.

Tulip growers longed to know what caused colour breaking. Aphids were seen to be in some way an agent for the desired effect so these destructive insects were actually encouraged.

In the 1930s, a virus was identified as causing 'broken' tulips. Spread by aphids, the virus caused the tulip's pigment to gather in particular areas. Modern growers dread the virus spreading through their tulips, so the old varieties of broken tulips – now known as 'Rembrandts' – are virtually obsolete.

Twentieth-century tulip varieties like 'Prince Carnival' and 'Esther Rijnveld' give the broken colour effect of the old Rembrandts, but are virus-free and safe to grow in the garden.

TULIPS IN THE GARDEN

The tulip is one of the easiest flowers to grow in the garden. Bulbs properly planted in well-drained soil are self-sufficient over the winter months. Unless attacked by pests or disease, most tulips bloom free from trouble.

The most popular tulips grown today are the Darwins, first developed in the late 19th century. Named in honour of the great theorist of natural selection, Darwins are hardy specimens indeed, long-lived both in the garden and as cut flowers.

The array of commercially available tulip varieties is tempting but bewildering to anyone thumbing through a modern bulb catalogue. For the sake of convenience, tulips are usually grouped according to blooming periods, which are spread over 12-14 weeks throughout the spring. An eclectic selection might progress in this way: At the beginning of April, '*T. kaufmanniana*', a native of Central Asia, is the first of the 'early tulips' to boom, opening its star-shaped blossoms to the warmth of the sun. It is followed by the classically

shaped single earlies, like the hot-pink
'Ibis' or blushing 'Apricot Beauty'.
'Oxford', one of the most popular
mid-season tulips, brings vivid scarlet to
the garden. 'My Lady', with
dreamy silver-green foliage
and coral petals, creates an
entirely different mood.
'Triumphs' appear in a wide range
of colours, including violet and purple.
The late season tulips offer some
dazzling, unusual varieties: the lily-flowered
tulips with narrow waists and pointed petals,
the fringed tulips with their serrated tips, and the
intriguing viridifloras, streaked with green. Double
'peony flowered' varieties sometimes seem unlike
tulips at all. The fantastic parrot tulips are the most
remarkable, with strangely twisted petals like the multi-
coloured feathers of exotic birds.

There are even some unusual fragrant tulip varieties:
the late bloomer 'Golden Show' has a strong, sweet scent.

THE BLACK TULIP

The idea of a black tulip, mysterious and dramatic, inspired Alexander Dumas, the author of *The Three Musketeers*, to write *La Tulipe Noire*. The hero, Cornelius Van Baerle, a Dutchman, is unjustly accused of treason against the Republic. Van Baerle, an expert tulip grower, is attempting to grow the elusive black tulip and when he is hauled off to prison hides his 'darling bulbs' next to his heart. He falls in love with his jailer's beautiful daughter and there follows a splendid tale of love and tulips.

In reality 'black' tulips are not black but deep maroon or deep purple.

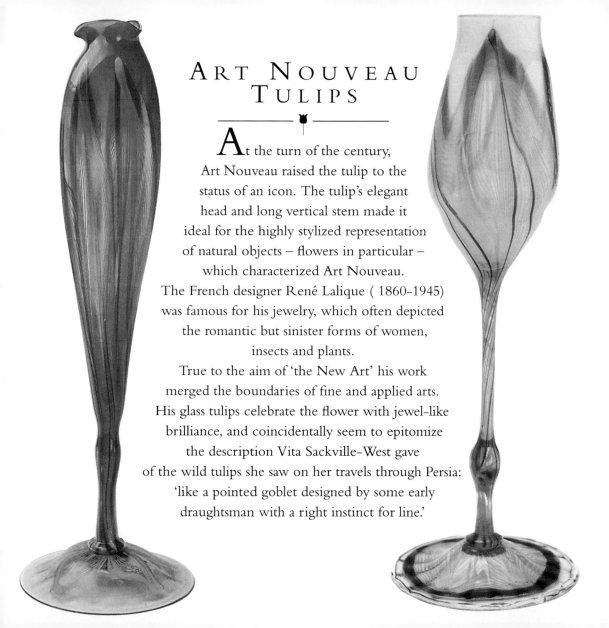

ART NOUVEAU TULIPS

At the turn of the century,
Art Nouveau raised the tulip to the
status of an icon. The tulip's elegant
head and long vertical stem made it
ideal for the highly stylized representation
of natural objects – flowers in particular –
which characterized Art Nouveau.
The French designer René Lalique (1860-1945)
was famous for his jewelry, which often depicted
the romantic but sinister forms of women,
insects and plants.
True to the aim of 'the New Art' his work
merged the boundaries of fine and applied arts.
His glass tulips celebrate the flower with jewel-like
brilliance, and coincidentally seem to epitomize
the description Vita Sackville-West gave
of the wild tulips she saw on her travels through Persia:
'like a pointed goblet designed by some early
draughtsman with a right instinct for line.'

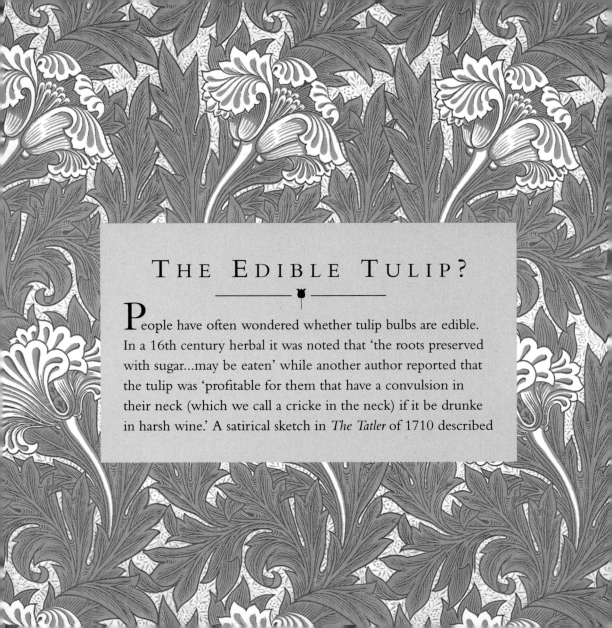

THE EDIBLE TULIP?

◆

People have often wondered whether tulip bulbs are edible. In a 16th century herbal it was noted that 'the roots preserved with sugar...may be eaten' while another author reported that the tulip was 'profitable for them that have a convulsion in their neck (which we call a cricke in the neck) if it be drunke in harsh wine.' A satirical sketch in *The Tatler* of 1710 described a tulip fancier whose cook had mistaken 'a handful of tulips for a heap of onions', and prepared 'a heap of pottage that cost me above a thousand pounds sterling.' Though they will never replace the potato, tulip bulbs were eaten in the Netherlands when food was scarce during the Second World War.

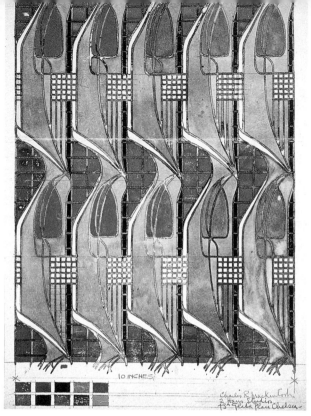

10 INCHES

Charles R. Mackintosh
2 Hans Studios
43ª Glebe Place Chelsea

A̲s then the Tulip from her morning sup
Of Heav'nly Vintage from the soil looks up
So you devoutly do the like, till Heav'n
To Earth invert you - like an empty cup.

From 'the Rubaiyat'
of Omar Khayyam (c. 1015-1123)

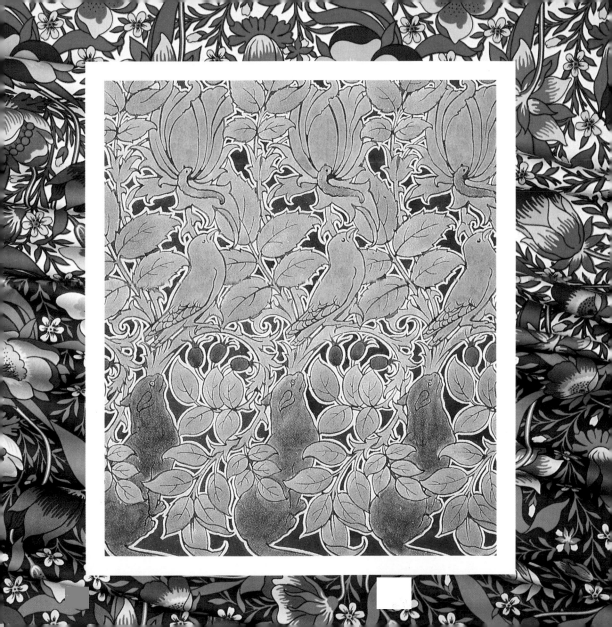

CUT TULIPS

It is a mistake to put cut tulips in the same vase with that other spring favourite, the daffodil. Although they look as if they belong together, their beauty is short-lived. Cut daffodils emit the gas ethylene (also produced by ripening fruit and cigarette smoke), as well as slime from their stems which kills the poor tulips. Instead of a vase of daffodils and tulips, achieve the same effect by combining red or pink single-blossomed tulips with a yellow double or frilled variety that mimics the daffodil.

There are some tricks that will extend the life of your cut tulips.

Beware buying tulips with heads that are either too young and green or already drooping. Plunge the stems into plenty of cool water as soon as possible, then trim the bottom of the stems on the diagonal.

Allow the flowers a good soak before arranging them in a clean vase large enough to allow the stems some room. Experts recommend adding a tiny drop of chlorine bleach to the water to inhibit bacterial growth.

The versatility of tulips makes them ideal for creative and unusual arrangements. A handful in a simple jug is charming, while an abundance of tulips is exuberant and impressive. With their flexible stems, tulips fit perfectly into a ring-shaped vase to make a centrepiece. For more elaborate displays, florists position tulips by running wire up the stems. Cooled candle wax may also be used to fix petals in place. Cut tulips last longest when kept in a cool room, but scented varieties need some warmth to bring out their fragrance.

When tulips are given in the Netherlands they are given in profusion – an unwritten social rule holds that proffering fewer than ten is miserly.

PENNSYLVANIA TULIPS

In the early days of North American settlement, colonists embarking on the long journey to the New World took care to pack things to remind them of home. Among these were tulip bulbs. As early as 1645, tulips were blooming in the tidy gardens of New Amsterdam, along what are now the bustling streets of New York. The first mayor of the city, Peter Stuyvesant, grew tulips in his garden, and we know from letters and journals that George Washington and Thomas Jefferson were also among the early Americans who grew tulips.

The Germans who settled the fertile valleys of Pennsylvania – the Pennsylvania 'Deutsch' or 'Dutch' – were farmers as well as skilled artisans. The tulip was a favourite and versatile motif in the hand-crafted domestic objects they made. It was painted on furniture, carved into wood, or reduced to a repeating pattern in patchwork quilts. The stylized tulip with three petals was regarded as a symbol of the Holy Trinity, and was often used in the elaborate decoration of important documents like birth and marriage certificates.

80   *La Tulipe*

TULIPA AND THE SULTAN

Tulips have inspired tales and legends such as the story of Tulipa, half-flower, half-woman. In his book *Les Fleurs Animées*, the French writer Albert Grandville tells how Tulipa, the beautiful daughter of a Dutch sea-captain, is captured by pirates. The pirates sell her to the Sultan Shahabaan but when he tires of her he has her sewn up in a sack and drowned in the Bosphorous.

This is based on the true story of Aimée Dubucq de Rivéry, a cousin of the Emperor Napoleon's wife, Josephine. Returning to France from the island of Martinique, the ship in which she was travelling was captured by Algerian pirates.

Aimée was offered to the Turkish Sultan, Abdul-Hamid I. He took her into his harem and she bore him a son. The birth was celebrated in 1783 by a great tulip festival and in time, Aimée grew to wield considerable power in Turkey. After the death of his father and his cousin – the next Sultan who was also Aimée's lover - her son reigned as Mahmud II.

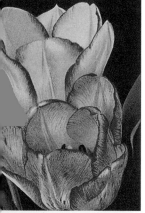

WHAT'S IN A NAME?

When de Busbecq wrote of the strange new flowers he had seen on his travels – 'those that the Turks call tulipam' – he was mistaken. He had probably misunderstood his guide's comparison of the flower's shape to that of a turban (*dulban*). The Turkish name for tulip is inherited from the Persian: *lalé*. Thus the period when the Ottoman court was obsessed with tulips is called the *Lalé Devir*, or tulip period.

What a vision is conjured up by the names of the tulip varieties of that time.

Beauty's Reward, Lover's Dream, Lightning Flash, Pink of Dawn, Heart Reviver and Ruby of Paradise are but a few of these

lyrically named Eastern blossoms.

A rather different sensibility prompted tulip names during the Dutch period of tulipmania. The 17th century was a golden age of prosperity in the Netherlands, thanks to a powerful navy and the riches gained through colonial trade. Little wonder that the names of the most expensive tulips of the day suggest a military bearing: Viceroy, Semper Augustus, General Bol and Admiral van Hoorn.

A look through a list of twentieth century tulip varieties reveals some evocative modern names. 'Elizabeth Arden' is a flattering lipstick red, 'Queen of the Night' tall and graceful in silky shades of purple, while a grouping of 'Mt. Tacoma' creates a flurry of white petals suggesting clouds and snow-capped peaks.

CONTAINER TULIPS

Tulips are the ideal container plant for those who have little space or no access to a garden. Almost any spot with adequate sunlight can be used. Courtyards, patios, steps and porches, balconies, roof gardens and of course that old favourite, the window sill, are all enlivened by a show of tulips.

The container should have adequate drainage, provided either by holes at the bottom or by a layer of pebbles or pottery shards. Container tulips which spend the winter outdoors need a good 3 inches (7.5 cm) of soil beneath the bulb to allow for adequate root growth, and at least 4 inches (10 cm) of soil on top.

Almost any container that is deep enough and provides adequate drainage can be used, allowing the creative gardener scope for experimentation.

Terracotta pots, wooden tubs, plastic window boxes, old metal troughs or even large baskets can be used. In areas with very severe winters, container tulips may be over-wintered in a garage or in a plunge bed filled with sand and covered with straw.

Planting the bulbs close together and in layers at different depths will give the container a natural, informal effect. Other plants can be added to the display: the small bulbs of muscari (grape hyacinth) and deep-blue scillas fit easily around the larger bulbs, while lobelias, primroses and pansies grow happily in containers and provide a low-growing counter-point to tall, brightly coloured tulips.

INDOOR TULIPS

Tulips may be 'forced' to bloom indoors by simulating outdoor growing conditions. A creative choice of container to complement your choice of tulips can help to make a stunning display. This old copper fish kettle works perfectly with the orange-yellow glow of these dwarf double tulips.

1.) Plant the bulbs in a well-drained container, close together but not touching, on a layer of bulb fibre at least as deep as the bulbs are high to allow room for root development. The tip of each bulb should be just above the surface.

2.) Water well and place in a cool position at a temperature no higher than 7°C (45°F). The container should be kept in a dark room or covered to keep out the light (black polythene is an ideal covering) for about ten weeks after planting. Keep the bulb fibre moist but don't over-water.

3.) When the stems have grown to a height of 2-3 inches (5-7.5cm), move the tulips to a warmer position – a temperature no higher than 18°C (65°F). Continue watering, and introduce the tulips gradually to normal daylight and average room temperature.

TULIP STENCILS AND DECOUPAGE

Tulips were hand-painted on furniture in Northern Europe during the 18th and 19th centuries, a folkart tradition that was carried to the American colonies. It is easy to create this picturesque look in your own home with tulip stencils.

To make a collection of tulip flowerpots, apply an undercoat of white emulsion to your terracotta pots, followed by several base coats of coloured emulsion. When this has dried, the base for your tulip stencils is ready. You can buy tulip stencils or make your own. Transfer your design onto stencil card and and cut it out with a craft knife. Tape the stencil in place and apply the paint with a gentle dabbing motion.

Craft shops sell fat bristle brushes and quick-drying paints specifically for stencilling.

To make Victorian-style découpage pots, cut out or photocopy old tulip illustrations and glue these firmly to a painted terracotta pot. Seal with several coats of varnish.

If you want to use your decorated terracotta pots as planters, protect the finish from water seeping through by coating the inside with oil-based paint, or use plastic plant pots inside them to hold plants and soil.

ARTIFICIAL TULIPS

Clean as a lady,
Cool as glass,
Fresh without fragrance
The tulip was.

The craftsman, who carved her
Of metal, prayed:
'Live oh thou lovely!'
Half metal she stayed.

'The Tulip' FROM KENSINGTON GARDENS
BY HUMBERT WOLFE.

Its graceful stems and shapely blossoms have made the tulip a favourite subject for reproduction. Fashioned in wood, paper, metal or latex, artificial tulips are effective in interior decoration. Stylish and sophisticated or charming and naive, craft tulips are a reminder of spring and a tribute to nature's art.

ENGLISH TULIPS –
'THE QUEEN OF BULBOUS FLOWERS'

The tulip was brought to England during the reign of Elizabeth I. Although it was at first 'a strange and forrein floure', it soon became essential to the English garden.

Universally commended 'for the stately aspect and for the admirable variety of colours', the tulip was praised as 'the Queen of all Bulbous Flowers.' Enthusiasm for the tulip even prompted one admirer to state that 'I do verily thinke that these are the Lilies of the field ...for these flours resemble lilies, and in these places where our Saviour was conversant they grow wilde in the fields'.

The tulip received royal approval when John Tradescant planted them in the gardens he designed for Charles I. As tulip varieties became more widely available, 'cottage tulips' sprang up in gardens throughout the country.

Exhibitions sponsored by tulip societies were a popular entertainment in the Victorian era. Amateur growers strove to produce tulips that met the exacting standards of the judges. The ideal English florists' tulip had to be rounded and open, 'shaped like a claret glass.' Today the tradition of the tulip show is carried on by the Wakefield and North of England Tulip society, founded in 1836, which holds its tulip show each spring.

TULIP FESTIVALS

The impulse to celebrate spring has made tulip festivals a centuries-old tradition. The grand tulip show at the Keukenhof gardens in Holland is famous, but tulip festivals are held around the world, thanks to Dutch settlers who planted tulips wherever they found a favourable climate. In England the flat sandy soil of Lincolnshire is ideal for tulips, and a thriving bulb industry was established near Spalding. Wonderful tulip floats and displays feature there each year in the

Springfields tulip festival.

In the United States, the annual tulip festival in Holland, Michigan opens with a ceremonial 'scrubbing of the streets' to celebrate the city's Dutch heritage.

Canada's biggest tulip festival, held in Ottawa, honours the birth of a Dutch princess while the Dutch royal family was in exile there during the Second World War.

While gardeners in the Northern hemisphere are preparing to plant their autumn bulbs, the tulip festivals 'down under' in Australia are just beginning.

The murmur of a cool stream
Bird song, ripe fruit in plenty
Bright multi-coloured tulips and fragrant roses.

'Gulistan' BY MUSHARRIFU'D-DIN SA'DI,
1258

Ladies, like variegated Tulips show;
'Tis to their Changes half their charms they owe.

ALEXANDER POPE (1688-1744)

The gardens fire with a joyful blaze
Of Tulips in the mornings' rays

RALPH WALDO EMERSON (1803-82)

The tulip white did for complexion seek,
And learned to interline its cheek;
Its onion root they then so high did hold,
That one was for a meadow sold.

'The Mower Against Gardens'
BY ANDREW MARVELL (1621-78)

TULIP

The tulips that have pushed a pointed tusk
In steady inches, suddenly resolve
Upon their gesture, earliest the royal
Princes of Orange and of Austria,
Their Courtier the little Duc de Thol,
And, since the State must travel with the Church,
In plum, shot crimson, couleur, Cardinal.

But grander than these dwarf diminutives,
Comes the tall Darwin with the waxing May,
Can stem so slender bear such sovereign head
Nor stoop with weight of beauty? See her pride
Equals her beauty, never grew so straight
A spire of faith, nor flew so bright a flag
Lacquered by brush strokes of the painting sun.

VITA SACKVILLE-WEST (1892–1962)

The tulip and the butterfly
Appear in gayer coats than I:
Let me be dressed fine as I will,
Flies, worms and flowers exceed me still

ISAAC WATTS (1674–1748)

THE LOVING TULIP

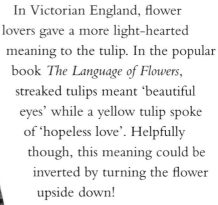

There is a romantic Persian folktale about tulips. Ferhad and Shirin were a couple who were tragically thwarted in love. When Ferhad received a false message that Shirin was dead, he was overcome with grief and plunged off a mountainside. Blood-red tulips sprang up where he died, as the poet Hafiz wrote:

And where the tulip, following close behind
The feet of Spring, her scarlet chalice rears
There Ferhad for the love of Shirin pined,
Dyeing the desert red with his heart's tears.

In 17th century Persia a gift of red tulips meant a young man wished to tell his beloved that he was 'on fire with her beauty'; and by the black base of it, that his heart was 'burnt to a coal.'

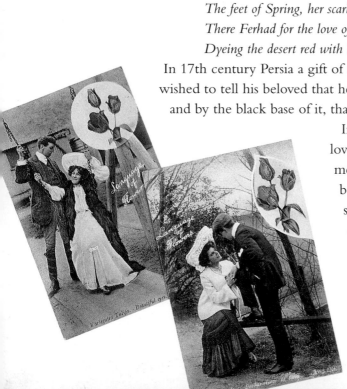

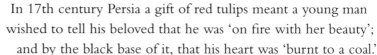

In Victorian England, flower lovers gave a more light-hearted meaning to the tulip. In the popular book *The Language of Flowers*, streaked tulips meant 'beautiful eyes' while a yellow tulip spoke of 'hopeless love'. Helpfully though, this meaning could be inverted by turning the flower upside down!

First published in Great Britain in 1994 by
Michael O'Mara Books Limited
9 Lion Yard, Tremadoc Road
London SW4 7NQ

A CIP catalogue record for this book is available from the British Library

ISBN 1–85479–949–5

10 9 8 7 6 5 4 3 2

Designed by Mick Keates
Text by Valerie Schloredt
Cover illustration by Tricia Newell

Printed and bound in Italy by New Interlitho

Acknowledgments

The publishers are grateful to the following for permission to reproduce illustrations:
The American Museum; pp. 42-43 The Bridgeman Art Library; p. 11, 20-21 Jane Churchill Limited;
pp. 8-9 ('Arles' fabric design), 58-59 ('St Remy', 'Tulip Squares' and 'Porcelain Garden' fabric designs)
Comstock; p. 45 (bottom) EWA; p. 38 (top), 50 Galerie Moderne, London; p. 30 The Garden Picture
Library: Lynne Brotchie; p. 40, Linda Burgess; pp. 2-3, 16-17, 36-37, 46-47 (middle), Mayer/Le Scanff;
p. 41 Sonia Halliday Photographs; pp. 14-15 Michael Harvey; p. 29 (arrangement by Jane Durbridge),
54 (papier mâché by Melanie Williams) International Flower Bulb Centre; p. 39 Sally Kindberg; p.25
(top) Liberty of London; p. 18 ('Alchemilla' furnishing design), 34-35 ('Nesfield' furnishing design),
63 ('Amelioras' furnishing design) Sue Miles & Mick Keates; p. 38 (bottom), 52, 57, 60 (top) Tricia
Newell; p. 45 (top) Clive Nichols; endpapers, p. 1, 24, 27, 48 (top) Amoret Tanner; p. 3 (top), 4 (top),
10 (bottom), 17, 28 (bottom right), 44, 46-47 (left and right), 53 (bottom left) Keith West; p. 26

A special thank you to Helen Hardy for the artificial flowers on pages 54-55, Sue Miles and Mick Keates
for the stencilled and découpage pots on pages 52-53, Melanie and Gerry Geenty for the cheese cooler
on page 55 and Derrick Witty for photography.